DEBT FREE!

A GUIDE TO FINANCIAL FREEDOM

Inspirational and Practical Advice to Conquer Debt

RAZANA GOBER

Debt Free! A Guide to Financial Freedom
Inspirational and Practical Advice to Conquer Debt
© 2025, Razana Gober

All rights reserved. No part of this publication may be reproduced, stored or transmitted in any form or by any means, electronic, mechanical, photocopying, recording, scanning, or otherwise without written permission from the publisher. It is illegal to copy this book, post it to a website, or distribute it by any other means without permission.

Publisher: Paris Press
Author: Razana Gober
Illustrations: Owned by Razana Gober
Published in the United States of America.
ISBN: 978-1-966915-02-7

No part of this publication may be reproduced, distributed, or transmitted in any form or by any means, including photocopying, recording, or other electronic or mechanical methods, without the prior written permission of the publisher, except in the case of brief quotations embodied in critical reviews and certain other noncommercial uses permitted by copyright law.

For permission requests, write to:
Email: razanaangel@yahoo.com
Instagram @razanagober LinkedIn: Razana Gober
Razana Gober asserts the moral right to be identified as the author of this work.

Designations used by companies to distinguish their products are often claimed as trademarks. All brand names and product names used in this book and on its cover are trade names, service marks, trademarks and registered trademarks of their respective owners. The publishers and the book are not associated with any product or vendor mentioned in this book. None of the companies referenced within the book have endorsed the book.

Disclaimer: This book is intended to provide helpful and informative material on the subjects addressed. It is not a substitute for professional advice. The author and publisher disclaim any liability arising from the use or application of the contents of this book.

This book is designed to provide accurate and authoritative information regarding the subject matter covered. It is sold with the understanding that the author and publisher are not engaged in rendering legal, financial, or other professional advice. If expert assistance is required, the services of a competent professional should be sought.

Dedication

To everyone who feels like they are drowning in debt: It is possible to be financially free, and I hope this book provides you with the knowledge, tools, and encouragement to reclaim your life.

Table of Contents

Introduction: Acknowledging Every Story *1*

Section 1: Foundations of Financial Freedom 5
- *Chapter 1: My Debt Story 7*
- *Chapter 2: Understanding Your Relationship with Money 11*
- *Chapter 3: Taking Accountability for Your Debt. 21*

Section 2: Building a Financial Plan 27
- *Chapter 4: Budgeting for Success 29*
- *Chapter 5: The Debt Snowball Method 35*
- *Chapter 6: Affordable Rewards 41*
- *Chapter 7: Saving While Paying Off Debt 49*
- *Chapter 8: Cost-Saving Tips 59*

Section 3: Increasing Income and Making Smart Choices 67
- *Chapter 9: Side Hustles and Increasing Income 69*
- *Chapter 10: Smart Financial Decisions 79*

Section 4: Navigating Complex Financial Challenges 87
- *Chapter 11: Handling Medical Debt 89*
- *Chapter 12: Creative Ways to Cut Costs 95*

Section 5: Maintaining Financial Freedom........ 105

Chapter 13: Staying Debt-Free............................. 107

Chapter 14: The Psychology of Debt-Free Living. 117

Chapter 15: How to Say No and Set Boundaries 125

Chapter 16: Financial Planning for Families 137

Chapter 17: Investing While Paying Off Debt..... 147

Section 6: Closing Inspiration............................ 157

Worksheets.. 159

Debt Tracking Worksheet 160

Monthly Budget Template 161

Debt Snowball Tracker.. 162

Savings Goal Chart... 163

Acknowledgments 165

Conclusion: Empowering Your Financial Journey
... 167

About the Author... 171

Introduction

Acknowledging Every Story

No Judgment, Just Hope

Everyone's story is different, and so is their financial situation. Debt doesn't discriminate—it affects people from all walks of life, and the reasons for being in debt are as varied as the people themselves. This book is not here to judge you. It's here to offer hope, guidance, and encouragement to help you take control of your finances, no matter your starting point.

I know what it feels like to be overwhelmed by debt. By the time COVID-19 hit, I was in over $60,000 of debt. I felt trapped and hopeless, not knowing how to dig my way out. I've worked minimum-wage jobs where the company didn't value me, the customers didn't appreciate me, and I felt invisible. I've applied to job after job, only to face rejection, even with a college degree in hand.

I know what it's like to be so broke that bread and eggs are all you can afford—breakfast, lunch, and dinner. I've worked overnight shifts, grabbed a couple of hours of sleep, and headed straight to my day job because the bills kept piling up. I know what it feels like to be drowning in debt, with no visible way out, and the stress of it all threatening to consume you.

I also understand that life's responsibilities make tackling debt even harder. Some people expect you to work two or three jobs to stay afloat, but what if you have kids to care for? A sick parent? A job that isn't flexible? What if working yourself into exhaustion just isn't sustainable?

Over the years, I've learned that while paying off debt is important, so is your health. You can't pour from an empty cup. Achieving financial freedom takes a balance of hard work, realistic planning, and self-care.

This book is my story and the lessons I've learned along the way. I hope it offers you not only practical strategies but also encouragement to take the first step toward a debt-free life. If I can do it, so can you.

Debt Free! A Guide to Financial Freedom

Section 1

Foundations of Financial Freedom

Chapter 1

My Debt Story

At one point in my life, I was drowning in over $60,000 of debt—and that didn't even include my student loans. Let me be clear: I didn't end up in that situation because I was reckless or living a life of luxury. My debt was accumulated over time from medical bills, dental bills, transportation costs, food, and other necessary expenses. It built up slowly, piece by piece, until I felt completely overwhelmed.

I'll never forget the weight of it. Every day felt like a losing battle. I was doing everything I could to stay afloat, but no matter how hard I tried, it seemed like I was running in place.

My First Car: A Hard Lesson

When I think back on those years, I remember the lessons I learned the hard way—starting with my first car. I bought that car outright with a combination of savings and a $2,000 loan from my father, who was alive at the time. I was determined to pay him back, and I did within six months. One of the most valuable pieces of advice my father gave me was to pay for car insurance in full to get the discount. That simple tip saved me money over the years, but it was just one of many lessons I had to learn.

The car itself, a Toyota Corolla, was far from ideal. I bought it from a dealership in Brooklyn, New York, where my brother-in-law worked at the time. Because of that connection, I trusted the dealership without question. Unfortunately, the car turned out to be a mess. The lights didn't work, and it wasn't safe to drive. Looking back, if I knew then what I know now, I would have never bought that car. But I didn't know better, and I made it work because I had no other choice.

That car may have been a headache, but it taught me a crucial lesson about the importance of doing research and asking questions before making financial decisions. Blind trust, even with good intentions, can lead to costly mistakes.

The Road to Freedom

Fast forward about ten years, and I can proudly say I am debt-free. That includes my student loans, which I paid off almost a year after getting married. I made a conscious decision to pay off my debts before I got married because I didn't want my husband to be responsible for the financial burdens I had created before we started our life together.

But let me be honest: the road to freedom wasn't easy. It required hard work, sacrifice, and a level of discipline I didn't know I had. I worked long hours, often taking on multiple jobs. I gave up things I wanted to buy and experiences I wanted to have because I knew they would set me back. There were days when all I could afford to eat were eggs and bread. I made egg and bread sandwiches for breakfast, lunch, and dinner. I worked overnight shifts, got a few hours of sleep, and went straight to my day job because the bills kept piling up.

A Hard-Fought Lesson

Through all of this, I learned the value of sacrifice and perseverance. Financial freedom doesn't happen overnight, and it certainly doesn't happen without effort. But every small step I took—whether it was paying off a credit card, skipping a dinner out, or picking up an extra shift—brought me closer to my goal.

There were moments when I wanted to give up. The stress was overwhelming, and the path ahead felt impossible. But I kept going. I reminded myself that I didn't want to spend the rest of my life chained to debt. I wanted peace of mind. I wanted freedom. And I knew I was the only one who could make it happen.

Today, I can proudly say that I've achieved what once felt impossible. My story is proof that no matter how deep in debt you are, with hard work, discipline, and a willingness to make sacrifices, you can take control of your finances and build a brighter future.

Chapter 2

Understanding Your Relationship with Money

Why It's Important

Your relationship with money is one of the most important factors in achieving financial success. It influences every financial decision you make, from how you spend and save to how you approach debt and investments. For many, debt isn't just a numbers problem—it's a mindset problem. Understanding and reshaping your beliefs about money is the foundation for long-term financial stability and freedom.

The Psychology Behind Money Habits

1. Emotional Spending Triggers

Many people spend money as a way to cope with emotions such as stress, boredom, or sadness. It's easy to rationalize purchases with thoughts like, "I deserve this" or "This will make me feel better." While retail therapy may provide temporary relief, it often leads to buyer's remorse and financial setbacks.

Ask Yourself:

- When do I tend to overspend? (e.g., after a stressful day, during celebrations, or when I feel bored).
- How do I feel after making impulsive purchases?

Practical Tip:

- Replace emotional spending with healthier coping mechanisms, such as going for a walk, calling a friend, or journaling about your feelings.

2. Scarcity vs. Abundance Mindset

If you constantly feel like there's "never enough money," you might be operating from a scarcity mindset. This mindset can lead to hoarding money or overspending out of fear of missing out. On the other hand, an abundance mindset helps you believe that financial opportunities are within reach, fostering smarter financial decisions.

Signs of a Scarcity Mindset:

- Fear of spending money, even on necessities.
- Feeling jealous of others' financial success.
- Believing you'll never get ahead, no matter how hard you try.

How to Shift to an Abundance Mindset:

- Celebrate small financial wins, such as paying off a credit card or saving $50.
- Surround yourself with positive financial influences, such as books, podcasts, or friends who inspire financial growth.
- Focus on what you can control, like creating a budget or increasing your income.

The Impact of Early Money Lessons

Your first experiences with money often shape your financial habits and beliefs. For example, if you grew up in a household where money was tight, you might associate money with stress or scarcity. Alternatively, if your family avoided talking about money, you might feel shame or confusion when managing your finances.

Foundations of Financial Freedom

Activity:

Take a few moments to reflect on these questions:

1. What is the first memory you have about money?
2. How did your parents or guardians handle money?
3. How have those experiences influenced your current financial habits?

Practical Tip:

If your early money lessons were negative, recognize that you have the power to change your narrative. Educate yourself about personal finance and practice small, consistent steps to build confidence in managing money.

Building Intentional Money Practices

Understanding your relationship with money isn't just about recognizing the problem—it's about taking actionable steps to create healthier habits.

1. Set Financial Boundaries

- ♦ Stop comparing yourself to others. Social media can make you feel like everyone is living their best life, but remember that people often only share their highlights—not their struggles.

- Avoid "lifestyle creep." Just because your income increases doesn't mean your spending should.

2. Create a Money Mission Statement

A money mission statement is a short statement that outlines your financial values and goals. It keeps you focused on what truly matters and helps you resist impulsive decisions.

Example:

"I value financial security and freedom. My goal is to live below my means, save for emergencies, and invest in my future."

3. Practice Gratitude

Regularly remind yourself of what you already have. Gratitude can shift your focus from what you lack to what you've accomplished, helping you feel more content and less tempted to overspend.

Activity: Mapping Your Money Personality

Use this activity to better understand your financial habits and how they impact your relationship with money:

1. What type of spender are you?

    - Impulsive spender
    - Emotional spender
    - Careful saver
    - Somewhere in between

2. What financial habits would you like to improve?

    - Spending less on non-essentials
    - Saving consistently
    - Reducing debt

3. What's one action you can take today to align your money habits with your goals?

Example Response:

    - "I'm an impulsive spender, and I want to save more consistently. Starting today, I'll set up an automatic transfer of $20 per week into my savings account."

Reframing Financial Failures

Mistakes are inevitable, but they don't define you. A missed payment or a financial misstep doesn't mean you've failed—it's an opportunity to learn and grow.

Steps to Reframe Financial Failures:

1. Acknowledge It Without Shame: Recognize the mistake and accept it as part of your journey.
2. Analyze What Went Wrong: Did you overspend because you didn't budget properly? Did an unexpected expense throw you off track?
3. Create a Plan to Prevent It in the Future: Use tools like reminders, a stricter budget, or an emergency fund to avoid repeating the mistake.

Final Thoughts

Understanding your relationship with money is a journey, not a destination. It requires self-reflection, honesty, and a commitment to change. The better you understand your habits and mindset, the easier it will be to make intentional financial decisions that align with your goals.

Money is a tool—not a source of stress or shame. By reshaping how you view and handle money, you can build a future of financial freedom, security, and peace of mind.

Chapter 3

Taking Accountability for Your Debt

Taking accountability for your debt is one of the most important steps in your journey to financial freedom. It doesn't matter how you ended up in this situation—what matters is deciding to take control now. This isn't about blaming yourself or feeling ashamed. It's about understanding where you stand so you can take the first steps toward living the life you deserve.

When I began this process, I knew it wasn't going to be easy. The first thing I did was take a deep breath. I braced myself for the numbers I was about to see, knowing I wouldn't like them. But as overwhelming as it was to confront my debt, I knew that seeing everything laid out in black and white was necessary. Without clarity, I couldn't create a game plan to move forward.

A Tough Lesson in Compassion

Years ago, I worked at a law firm that specializes in debt collection. I absolutely hated that job. Every day, I felt like a little piece of my soul was being chipped away. One call, in particular, changed everything for me.

I was speaking with a woman who had lost her husband and son in a fire that had burned her home to the ground. She was drowning in debt, and as she told me her story, I felt compelled to verify it. I Googled her case, and everything she said was true.

All I wanted to do was help her. I couldn't bring her family back, but I wanted to forgive her debt and give her some peace. I spoke to my supervisor, but even after hearing the details of her tragedy, I was told to set up a payment plan with her. That night, I went home and cried. I realized then that the place I worked at had no heart, and I couldn't stay there any longer. I handed in my two weeks' notice and left for a new career in a new city.

I'm sharing this story because I want you to know that debt doesn't define who you are. Life happens. Circumstances beyond your control can lead to financial hardship. What matters now is taking accountability—not as a punishment, but as an act of empowerment.

Taking Inventory

When I started tackling my debt, I began by taking inventory of everything I owed. I wrote down every financial obligation—every credit card (open and closed), every medical and dental bill, and even small subscriptions. If a credit card account had been closed for years, I requested a letter from the creditor confirming the account was closed and the balance was paid in full. I didn't want to risk being held accountable for a debt I didn't owe.

I also included personal loans from family and friends. If I had borrowed money from my parents, siblings, or anyone else, it went on the list. My goal was to pay back every penny I owed.

Here's how I tracked my debts:

- The name of the creditor
- The due date for payments
- The interest rate
- The minimum payment amount
- The total amount owed

The Long Journey

This wasn't a one-time effort. I kept track of my debts every single month. At the end of the month, I would review my progress. At the beginning of the month, I would set my plan for the weeks ahead. I did this diligently for years, and eventually, it worked.

I started with the smallest balances first. Paying off a smaller debt gave me a sense of accomplishment and the momentum to tackle larger ones. But it wasn't always a smooth journey. There were times when I paid off a credit card only to have the balance rise back up again.

Life has a way of throwing unexpected challenges at you. Sometimes my car would break down. Other times, I couldn't afford my school books or groceries, and I had to use my credit card just to get by. This cycle continued for years, mainly because I didn't have a good-paying job. Even working two minimum-wage jobs wasn't enough to cover everything.

Perseverance Pays Off

Despite the setbacks, I kept going. Month after month, I tracked my debts, updated my records, and stuck to my plan. Slowly but surely, the balances began to shrink. It wasn't easy. It required discipline, patience, and a lot of sacrifice. But in the end, it worked.

Taking accountability for your debt doesn't mean you'll have all the answers right away, and it doesn't mean the journey will be free of setbacks. But it's the first step toward taking control of your finances. Once you know exactly where you stand, you can begin to take action—and every small step forward will bring you closer to financial freedom.

Section 2

Building a Financial Plan

Chapter 4

Budgeting for Success

In every story I've heard about people getting out of debt, there's always one common element: a budget. Budgeting is the backbone of any successful debt payoff plan. It's not just about numbers—it's about knowing exactly where your money is going, staying disciplined, and having a clear path toward your goals.

When I started my debt-free journey, I lived on a very strict budget. I gave myself little to no "play money" because I knew that one day, the sacrifice would be worth it. I told myself that if I stayed disciplined now, I'd eventually have all the financial freedom I wanted.

The Power of Awareness

A budget isn't just a list of numbers; it's a tool that gives you clarity and control. By tracking your income and expenses, you become fully aware of where your money is going and how much you're spending. That awareness is key to making smarter decisions.

For example, treating yourself to a coffee, a meal, or even a trip isn't a bad thing—but if you're not aware of how those small expenses add up, they can derail your progress. Budgeting isn't about depriving yourself; it's about making intentional choices that align with your goals.

Tracking Every Penny

I tracked every expense—from bills and household items to transportation—down to the last penny. I knew I had no choice but to be meticulous. My income was limited, and every dollar needed to be accounted for.

I lived like that for a very long time, not because I wanted to but because I had to. And while it was challenging at first, it became second nature over time. Today, that habit has become one of my greatest strengths. Because I practiced budgeting for so many years, I feel comfortable managing my finances now.

The Budgeting Process

Here's how I approached budgeting:

1. Write Everything Down: Start by listing all your expenses, no matter how small. Include fixed costs like rent, utilities, and transportation, as well as variable costs like groceries, dining out, and entertainment.
2. Set Spending Limits: Allocate specific amounts for each category based on your income and goals. Be realistic but firm—your budget should reflect your priorities.
3. Track Your Progress: At the end of the month, review your actual spending versus your budget. Adjust as needed and identify areas where you can improve.
4. Stay Consistent: Budgeting is not a one-time activity; it's a habit. Whether you review your budget weekly or monthly, make it a regular part of your routine.

Personal Story: The Strict Budget

During the years I worked to pay off my debt, my budget was my lifeline. I didn't give myself much room for extras because I knew every dollar counted. I skipped the coffee runs, avoided dining out, and said no to things I wanted but didn't need.

It wasn't easy. There were times when I wanted to splurge or treat myself, but I kept reminding myself of the bigger picture. I wanted to be debt-free. I wanted the peace of mind that comes with financial freedom. So, I stuck to my plan, knowing that the sacrifices I was making were temporary and would pay off in the long run.

Practical Tips for Budgeting

- Use a System That Works for You: Whether it's a spreadsheet, a budgeting app, or pen and paper, find a system that's easy to use and stick with it.
- Be Honest with Yourself: Don't underestimate your expenses or overestimate your income. A realistic budget is more effective than a perfect one.
- Build Flexibility Into Your Budget: Life happens. Set aside a small amount for

unexpected expenses so you're not caught off guard.

A Lifelong Skill

Budgeting isn't just a tool for paying off debt—it's a skill that will serve you for the rest of your life. By practicing discipline and consistency, you're not just getting out of debt; you're building a foundation for long-term financial stability.

Chapter 5

The Debt Snowball Method

The Debt Snowball Method is one of the most popular and effective strategies for paying off debt. It focuses on tackling the smallest debts first, regardless of interest rate, to build momentum and keep you motivated.

Why It Works

Paying off small debts quickly gives you a sense of accomplishment. This psychological boost keeps you going, even when the overall journey feels daunting. Every time you eliminate a debt, it's a reminder that you're capable of making progress.

That feeling of success builds momentum and fuels your determination to tackle larger balances.

It's also OK to treat yourself when you accomplish something, like paying off a balance on a credit card—as long as you have the cash to do it. I'll admit, I treated myself along the way. Sometimes it was dinner, other times a nice shirt, but those small rewards were my way of acknowledging my progress. I don't regret it because it kept me motivated. It was my one good thing for the month, and I was proud of it.

Steps to Use the Debt Snowball Method

1. List All Your Debts:Include the balance, interest rate, and minimum payment for each.
2. Organize Your Debts:Arrange them from smallest to largest balance, regardless of the interest rate.
3. Focus on the Smallest Debt: Pay as much as you can toward the smallest debt while making minimum payments on the others.
4. Snowball the Payments:Once the smallest debt is paid off, apply the amount you were paying toward it to the next smallest debt.

Repeat this process until all debts are paid off.

Personal Story

After years of being in debt, I'll never forget the feeling of paying off my first major balance. It was a $5,000 debt, and when I made that final payment, it felt like a huge weight had been lifted off my shoulders.

I was so proud of myself that I put the card away and didn't touch it for a long time because I was terrified of falling back into the same trap. Unfortunately, life has a way of throwing challenges at you, and eventually, I did end up using the card again.

I don't remember exactly what the expense was, but I know it wasn't for a vacation, luxury items, or partying. It was something necessary, something I couldn't afford to pay for in cash because I didn't have an emergency fund. At that time, the credit card became my emergency fund.

That experience taught me the importance of having savings while paying off debt. Without a safety net, even the smallest unexpected expense can set you back. But I didn't let that setback stop me. I picked myself up and started over, determined to make progress once again.

Activity: Organize Your Debts for the Snowball Method

Use the following framework to organize your debts. Include details such as the creditor's name, the total balance, interest rate, due date, and minimum payment. This clarity will help you stay focused and track your progress:

Creditor	Interest Rate	Due Date	Minimum Payment	Total Balance
Credit Credit A	19.99%	5th	$25	$500
Medical Bill	0%	10th	$50	$1,200
Car Loan	8%	20th	$250	$5,000

Sometimes all you can do is make the minimum payment—and that's OK. What matters is that you're staying on top of your obligations and moving forward.

Tips for Staying Motivated

- Celebrate Small Wins: Reward yourself each time you pay off a debt. Choose a budget-friendly treat, like a special meal or a new shirt, to mark the occasion.
- Track Your Progress: Keep a visual chart of your debt payoff journey. Watching the balances shrink can be incredibly motivating.
- Stay Focused on Your Goal: Remind yourself why you're doing this—whether it's to buy a home, save for retirement, or simply achieve peace of mind.

The Debt Snowball Method is powerful because it's about more than just numbers—it's about building confidence and keeping momentum. Every step, no matter how small, brings you closer to your goal of financial freedom.

Chapter 6

Affordable Rewards

Celebrating milestones is an essential part of staying motivated on your journey to financial freedom. Rewards don't have to be extravagant or expensive—they just need to be meaningful and within your budget. Recognizing your progress keeps you focused, energized, and inspired to continue moving forward.

Why Rewards Matter

When you achieve a goal, it's important to take a moment to acknowledge your hard work. Celebrating your progress gives you a sense of accomplishment and reinforces positive habits. This reminder of your success can help you stay motivated for the next step in your journey.

It's easy to feel like you need to deprive yourself while paying off debt, but small, intentional rewards can provide a much-needed boost. The key is to keep these rewards budget-friendly and aligned with your overall financial goals.

Personal Story: Celebrating Small Wins

After paying off one of my credit cards, I decided to treat myself to a facial I found on Groupon. It wasn't an extravagant expense, but it was a small indulgence that reminded me I was making progress. That moment felt like a turning point—it gave me confidence that my sacrifices were paying off and that I was on the right track.

Setting aside a small portion of my budget for rewards kept me motivated and prevented feelings of burnout. I didn't feel deprived because I was still able to enjoy little things along the way.

Budget-Friendly Reward Ideas

Here are some affordable ways to celebrate your milestones without derailing your financial progress:

Building a Financial Plan

1. Self-Care

   - Treat yourself to a DIY spa day at home with candles, face masks, and soothing music.
   - Invest in a small item for your favorite hobby, like new paints, yarn, or gardening tools.
   - Buy a book you've been wanting to read or revisit a favorite classic.

2. Entertainment

   - Host a movie night at home with your favorite snacks and cozy blankets.
   - Look for discounted tickets to a local theater, concert, or comedy show.
   - Try a free or low-cost online class to learn a new skill or hobby.

3. Travel

   - Plan a day trip to a nearby park, beach, or hiking trail. Pack a picnic and enjoy the scenery.
   - Use travel deal websites like Groupon or Hopper to book a budget-friendly weekend getaway.

- Explore your local area as if you were a tourist—visit landmarks, museums, or hidden gems.

4. Food and Dining

- Visit your favorite café for a treat, like a coffee or dessert.
- Try a new recipe and cook a special dinner at home. Light candles and make it feel like a fancy restaurant experience.
- Host a themed potluck with friends where everyone contributes a dish.

5. Fitness and Wellness

- Take a yoga class or try a workout class you've never done before.
- Splurge on a small piece of fitness equipment, like resistance bands or a jump rope.
- Go for a relaxing walk or bike ride in a scenic location.

6. Creative Rewards

- Create a vision board to celebrate your progress and visualize your next goals.
- Start a scrapbook or journal documenting your debt-free journey.

Building a Financial Plan

- Spend an afternoon on a creative project, like painting, knitting, or baking.

7. Budget-Friendly Shopping

- Shop at a thrift store for a unique find, like a new outfit or home decor item.
- Wait for sales or clearance events to buy something you've been eyeing.
- Treat yourself to a small but meaningful purchase, like a scented candle or a new notebook.

Tips for Rewarding Yourself

1. Set Aside a Reward Fund:

Budget a small portion of your monthly income for rewards. Even $10–$20 can go a long way toward affordable treats.

2. Tie Rewards to Specific Milestones:

Celebrate each paid-off debt or other financial achievement with a designated reward. This will give you something to look forward to as you progress.

3. Keep It Budget-Friendly:
Remember, the goal is to celebrate without undoing your progress. Choose rewards that fit your budget and bring you joy.

Activity: Plan Your Rewards

Use the table below to brainstorm affordable rewards for your milestones:

Milestone	Reward	Budget
Paid off Car	Budget-friendly weekend getaway	$300
Paid off credit cards	Dinner out	$50
Met my goal for emergency fund	Buy a new outfit	$50

Revisit this table as you make progress. Having planned rewards will keep you excited and focused on your financial goals.

Final Thought

Celebrating milestones is a powerful way to stay motivated on your journey to financial freedom. By choosing meaningful and budget-friendly rewards, you can enjoy the process and stay inspired without compromising your progress. Every small win deserves recognition—because you're creating a brighter, more secure future with every step forward.

Chapter 7

Saving While Paying Off Debt

Many people assume that if they're in debt, they can't afford to save. However, building a small savings cushion is essential to prevent unexpected expenses from derailing your progress. Even saving a little bit at a time can make a significant difference in the long run.

Saving while paying off debt may feel counterintuitive, but it's one of the smartest financial decisions you can make. It not only helps you stay prepared for emergencies but also keeps you from falling back into the cycle of debt.

Why Saving Matters

Emergencies are inevitable—whether it's a car repair, a medical expense, or a sudden job loss. Without savings, many people turn to credit cards or loans to cover these unexpected costs, which can erase months of progress.

By saving while paying off debt, you create a safety net that protects you from financial setbacks. Even small contributions provide a sense of security, empowering you to handle unexpected challenges without derailing your financial goals.

Personal Story: How My Emergency Fund Saved Me

When COVID-19 hit, my industry shut down completely, and I couldn't work. To make matters worse, unemployment benefits were delayed for months. Thankfully, I had been saving a small portion of my income each month. My emergency fund allowed me to cover my basic expenses for four months until I received my first unemployment check.

Without that savings cushion, I would have had no choice but to rely on credit cards, putting myself back into debt. That experience solidified my belief in the importance of saving, even when paying off debt. Life is unpredictable, and having a financial buffer can make all the difference.

Tips for Saving While Paying Off Debt

1. Start Small:

    - Saving doesn't have to be overwhelming. Begin with $10–$20 a week. Over time, these small contributions add up and can provide peace of mind.

2. Automate Your Savings:

    - Set up automatic transfers to a separate savings account. Automation removes the temptation to skip saving and ensures consistency.

3. Treat Savings Like a Bill:

    - Include savings as a line item in your budget, just like rent or utilities. Prioritizing savings helps you stay consistent, even when money is tight.

4. Use Windfalls Wisely:

    - When you receive unexpected income—such as tax refunds, bonuses, or cash gifts—allocate a portion toward savings and debt repayment.

5. Cut Back Temporarily:
    - Identify areas in your budget where you can reduce spending temporarily. For example, skip dining out or cancel non-essential subscriptions and redirect those funds toward savings.

6. Take on a Side Hustle:
    - Consider freelance work, tutoring, rideshare driving, or selling items you no longer need. Use the extra income to build your emergency fund.

7. Use Cashback Apps and Rewards:
    - Apps like Ibotta, Fetch Rewards, and Rakuten can help you earn cashback on everyday purchases. Deposit those savings into your emergency fund.

8. Set Specific Goals:
    - Break your savings target into smaller, manageable milestones. For example, aim to save $500, then $1,000, and so on.

Building a Financial Plan

9. Avoid Dipping Into Savings:
    - ♦ Commit to only using your emergency fund for true emergencies, such as medical bills or car repairs—not discretionary spending.

Activity: Calculate Your Emergency Fund Goal

Use the following table to determine how much you need for a fully funded emergency fund based on your monthly expenses:

Expense	Monthly Amount	3-Month Goal	6-Month Goal
Rent/Mortgage			
Utilities			
Groceries			
Transportation			
Health Insurance			
Car Insurance			
Misc			
Total			

Building a Financial Plan

Practical Steps to Add to Savings When Ends Don't Meet

If you're struggling to make ends meet, here are some creative ways to grow your savings:

1. Sell Unused Items:

- Declutter your home and sell items you no longer need on platforms like eBay, Facebook Marketplace, or Poshmark.

2. Embrace DIY Solutions:

- Learn to do simple repairs, cook meals at home, and make your own cleaning supplies to save money.

3. Cancel Non-Essential Subscriptions:

- Temporarily pause streaming services, gym memberships, or other non-essential expenses to free up funds for savings.

4. Participate in Community Resources:

- Look for free local resources like food banks, clothing drives, or community assistance programs to reduce living expenses.

5. Round Up Your Purchases:

    ♦ Use apps like Acorns or Chime that round up your purchases to the nearest dollar and deposit the difference into your savings.

6. Negotiate Your Bills:

    ♦ Call your utility providers, insurance companies, or phone carriers to negotiate better rates or explore alternative plans.

7. Find Free Entertainment:

    ♦ Take advantage of free events, library resources, and outdoor activities instead of spending on costly entertainment.

8. Embrace Meal Prep:

    ♦ Plan your meals in advance to save on dining out and reduce food waste.

Final Thought

Saving while paying off debt may feel challenging, but it's one of the smartest financial decisions you can make. Building even a small savings cushion provides a sense of security, protects you from unexpected expenses, and prevents setbacks on your debt-free journey.

Remember, every dollar saved brings you closer to your goals. With a little discipline, creativity, and persistence, you can create a solid financial foundation that supports your dreams and safeguards your future.

Chapter 8

Cost-Saving Tips

Saving money doesn't mean giving up everything you enjoy. It's about being resourceful, intentional, and making smart choices that align with your financial goals. Small, consistent changes can add up to significant savings over time, helping you stay on track while still enjoying life in meaningful ways.

My Story: Budgeting to the Last Penny

When I was deep in debt, I had to budget down to the last penny. Going out for a $30 meal wasn't an option. I cooked all my meals at home, and meal prepping became a necessity, especially when I was on the road for work. Instead of joining coworkers at nice restaurants, I'd stop by a grocery store and pick up practical, budget-friendly meals.

It wasn't easy. Watching others live carefree while I stuck to a strict budget was difficult, but I reminded myself that my sacrifices were temporary. Today, I can say with confidence that it was all worth it. I no longer have to deal with debt payments, and the discipline I developed has made me more financially resilient.

Practical Ways to Save Money

Here are tips to help you save on everyday expenses, no matter your income level:

1. Groceries:

- Shop at discount stores like Aldi, Lidl, or Walmart.
- Use apps like Ibotta, Fetch Rewards, or Rakuten for cashback and rebates.
- Plan meals for the week and create a shopping list to avoid unnecessary purchases.
- Buy in bulk for staples like rice, pasta, beans, and canned goods.

Building a Financial Plan

- Take advantage of BOGO deals (Buy One, Get One Free) and stock up on non-perishable items.
- Opt for store brands—they're often as good as name brands but significantly cheaper.

2. Household Supplies:

- Use reusable items, like microfiber cloths instead of paper towels.
- Buy cleaning supplies and household goods during sales or clearance events.
- Shop at dollar stores for basic household items like sponges, detergents, and trash bags.

3. Utilities:

- Switch to energy-efficient LED bulbs to lower electricity costs.
- Unplug electronics when not in use to reduce "phantom energy" consumption.
- Use a programmable thermostat to save on heating and cooling bills.
- Wash clothes in cold water and air dry them to cut down on energy costs.

4. Transportation:

- Carpool with coworkers or friends to save on gas.
- Use public transportation if it's available and affordable in your area.
- Keep your tires properly inflated and follow a regular maintenance schedule to improve fuel efficiency.

5. Entertainment:

- Look for free events in your community, such as outdoor concerts, festivals, or museum days.
- Host potlucks or game nights instead of dining out with friends.
- Cancel unused subscriptions or share streaming services with friends and family to split the cost.

6. Clothing and Accessories:

- Shop secondhand at thrift stores, consignment shops, or online platforms like Poshmark.
- Wait for seasonal sales or clearance events to buy clothing.
- Organize clothing swaps with friends or family to refresh your wardrobe for free.

Building a Financial Plan

7. Personal Care:

- Learn how to do simple grooming tasks yourself, such as cutting your hair or doing your nails.
- Make DIY beauty products, like sugar scrubs or face masks, using ingredients you already have at home.
- Use coupons for toiletries and personal care items, and stock up during sales.

8. Dining Out:

- Limit eating out to special occasions and budget for it in advance.
- Split meals or order appetizers instead of full entrees to save money.
- Take advantage of happy hour discounts or daily specials.

9. Technology:

- Buy refurbished electronics instead of brand-new ones.
- Use free software alternatives for paid apps and programs.
- Wait for major sale events, like Black Friday or Cyber Monday, to purchase gadgets.

10. General Savings Tips:

- Always shop with a list to avoid impulse purchases.
- Use cashback credit cards responsibly to earn rewards on purchases you already planned to make.
- Delay non-essential purchases by 24–48 hours to decide if you truly need them.

Building a Financial Plan

Activity: Create Your Cost-Saving Plan

Use this template to brainstorm and track your cost-saving strategies:

Category	Expense	Savings Strategy	Estimated Savings
Groceries	Weekly groceries	Use coupons, shop store brands, meal prep	$20/week
Utilities	Electricity	Switch to LED bulbs, unplug devices	$15/month
Transportation	Gas	Carpool, check tire pressure	$10/week

Revisit this table monthly to update your strategies and track how much you're saving. Adjust your approach as needed to maximize your results.

Final Thoughts

Saving money doesn't mean sacrificing your quality of life—it's about being intentional and making small, practical changes that align with your financial goals. Remember, every dollar you save is a step closer to financial freedom. Even on a tight budget, you can find ways to enjoy life while securing your financial future.

Section 3

Increasing Income and Making Smart Choices

Chapter 9

Side Hustles and Increasing Income

Why It's Important:

When you're trying to pay off debt, cutting costs alone may not be enough. Increasing your income through side hustles or other opportunities can accelerate your journey, help you build a financial safety net, and provide breathing room for unexpected expenses.

Side hustles offer flexibility, creativity, and an opportunity to use your skills to boost your income. Even a few extra hours a week can make a significant difference in your financial progress.

Personal Story: Working as an Overnight Monitor

During my debt-free journey, I worked as an overnight monitor for several years. The hours were long and often grueling, but the steady income helped me stay afloat while chipping away at my debt. It wasn't glamorous, but it was worth it. That extra job gave me the financial flexibility I needed to pay my bills and even save a little along the way.

This experience taught me the value of hard work and the importance of taking opportunities that align with your financial goals—even if they're not ideal.

20 Side Hustle Ideas to Increase Income

Here are 20 practical side hustles that can help you boost your income while maintaining flexibility:

1. Night Monitor/Overnight Shift Work

- ♦ Great for people with flexible schedules who don't mind unconventional hours.

Increasing Income and Making Smart Choices

2. Freelance Writing or Editing

- Use platforms like Upwork or Fiverr to find clients. You can write blog posts, edit resumes, or proofread documents.

3. Tutoring

- Offer tutoring services in subjects you excel at, either in person or online through platforms like Tutor.com or VIPKid.

4. Rideshare Driving

- Drive for Uber or Lyft during your free time. Weekend and evening hours often yield higher earnings.

5. Food Delivery

- Deliver food through apps like DoorDash, Uber Eats, or Grubhub.

6. Pet Sitting or Dog Walking

- Apps like Rover and Wag make it easy to find pet-sitting gigs. This is perfect if you love animals.

7. Selling Handmade Goods

- Use Etsy to sell crafts, jewelry, art, or home decor items.

8. Virtual Assistance
    - Help small businesses with tasks like email management, scheduling, or social media through remote work platforms.

9. Babysitting/Nannying
    - Offer childcare services to families in your area, either occasionally or regularly.

10. House Sitting
    - Watch over homes for people who are traveling. This can include taking care of plants, mail, and pets.

11. Transcription Work
    - Sign up with platforms like Rev or TranscribeMe to earn money transcribing audio files.

12. Teaching English Online*
    - Platforms like VIPKid or Cambly allow you to teach English to students around the world.

13. Social Media Management
    - Many small businesses need help managing their online presence. Offer your skills to

Increasing Income and Making Smart Choices

create posts, manage ads, and engage with followers.

14. Selling Items Online
    - Declutter your home and sell items you no longer need on eBay, Poshmark, or Facebook Marketplace.

15. Yard Work or Landscaping
    - Offer lawn care, gardening, or snow-shoveling services in your neighborhood.

16. Freelance Graphic Design
    - If you have design skills, create logos, flyers, or social media graphics for businesses.

17. Photography
    - Offer photography services for events or sell stock photos on platforms like Shutterstock or Adobe Stock.

18. Event Staffing
    - Bartend, cater, or help with setup and cleanup for weddings or parties. These gigs are often available on weekends.

19. Car Detailing
    - Provide affordable car cleaning and detailing services in your community.

20. Renting Out a Room or Space

- ♦ Use Airbnb to rent out a spare room, garage, or even your driveway for extra income.

How to Find the Right Side Hustle for You

1. Assess Your Skills and Interests

- ♦ What are you good at? What do you enjoy doing? Choosing a side hustle that aligns with your strengths will make the work more enjoyable and sustainable.

2. Consider Your Schedule

- ♦ Look for opportunities that fit into your existing commitments. For example, overnight shifts may work if your days are busy, or online work might suit you if you have limited transportation options.

3. Start Small

- ♦ You don't need to dive in full-time. Start with a few hours a week to see if the side hustle fits your lifestyle.

4. Focus on Flexibility

- ♦ Many side hustles, like freelancing or gig work, allow you to choose your hours. This is especially helpful if you're balancing other responsibilities.

5. Use Online Platforms
- Websites like Upwork, Fiverr, TaskRabbit, and Rover can connect you with clients and job opportunities.

Maximizing Side Hustle Earnings

1. Set Clear Goals:
- Decide how much extra income you want to earn each month and how you'll use it (e.g., debt repayment, savings).

2. Create a Dedicated Schedule:
- Set aside specific times to work on your side hustle to maintain consistency without overworking yourself.

3. Reinvest in Your Hustle:
- If applicable, invest in tools, education, or marketing to grow your side hustle. For example, upgrade your equipment if you're a photographer or take an online course to expand your skills.

4. Track Your Earnings and Expenses:

- ♦ Keep detailed records for tax purposes and ensure you're making a profit after deducting expenses like gas, supplies, or platform fees.

Why Side Hustles Are Worth It

Side hustles are more than just a source of extra income—they're an opportunity to build skills, explore new passions, and take control of your financial future. They can also provide a safety net, offering financial stability during uncertain times or when unexpected expenses arise.

Even if it's not easy at first, the extra effort can pay off significantly in the long run. Whether you're earning an extra $200 or $2,000 a month, every dollar helps you get closer to becoming debt-free and financially secure.

Final Thought

Your time is valuable, so choose a side hustle that aligns with your goals, interests, and schedule. While the extra hours may feel overwhelming at times, remind yourself of the bigger picture: you're investing in a brighter, debt-free future.

With hard work, discipline, and the right strategy, your side hustle can help you pay off debt faster, build savings, and create financial opportunities you never thought possible.

Chapter 10

Smart Financial Decisions

Making smart financial decisions is critical for reducing debt and creating long-term stability. Some of the most impactful choices you'll make involve major expenses, such as buying a car or a home. These decisions can have a lasting effect on your financial health, so it's essential to weigh the pros and cons and align your choices with your goals.

Buying vs. Leasing a Car

When it comes to transportation, deciding whether to buy or lease a car can significantly affect your finances. Here's an overview of each option:

Leasing a Car:

- Lower monthly payments, but you never gain ownership of the car.
- Mileage limits and potential fees for excess wear and tear.
- Constant payments since you're essentially renting the car.

Buying a Car:

- Higher upfront costs, but you save more in the long run.
- No mileage limits or restrictions once the car is paid off.
- The car becomes an asset you can sell or trade later.

My Perspective:

While I've never leased a car, I know many people who have, and I firmly believe it's a waste of money. When you lease, you're essentially renting the car, and at the end of the term, you have nothing to show for the money you've spent.

My First Car: A Hard Lesson

My first car was a beat-up Toyota that I bought with cash for a couple of thousand dollars. It wasn't fancy, and it had its share of problems, but it got me where I needed to go. Most importantly, I didn't have a car payment. For years, I drove that car and avoided taking on unnecessary debt.

Eventually, I decided to buy a car with a payment, thinking it would make me feel more like an adult. My sister and her then-husband had told me that "adults have payments," and I let that influence my decision. I'll never forget that moment—it taught me a valuable lesson about making financial decisions based on my own goals, not societal expectations.

Renting vs. Buying a Home

Housing is one of the largest expenses in any budget. Deciding whether to rent or buy depends on your financial situation, lifestyle, and long-term goals.

Renting:

- Flexibility to move without long-term commitments.
- Lower upfront costs but no equity built.
- Rent increases over time, leaving you with higher living expenses.

Buying a Home:

- ♦ Higher upfront costs, but you build equity over time.
- ♦ Stable monthly payments with a fixed mortgage.
- ♦ Responsibility for maintenance, property taxes, and repairs.

Personal Story:

I rented for years, and while it allowed me to move around quite a bit, I never truly felt at home. I've always wanted to own a home so I could make it my own—whether it was painting the walls or making changes without needing a landlord's permission.

For a while, I shared a home with a group of roommates who were also flight attendants and pilots. It worked out well because we were rarely home at the same time. That arrangement saved me a lot of money. While it's not practical for everyone, especially if you have a family, it suited my situation at the time because I was single, unattached, and didn't have children yet.

Things changed after I got married and found out I was pregnant. My husband and I decided it was time to start looking at houses—not necessarily to buy immediately, but to get an idea of what we wanted. By that point, I had paid off all my debt except for my student loans, which I cleared shortly after my son was born.

Tips for Smart Home Buying

1. Negotiate the Price:

- Don't settle for the listing price. Research the market, compare similar homes, and use that information to negotiate with the seller.
- Request seller concessions, such as covering closing costs or including appliances.

2. Buy Down the Interest Rate:

- Ask your lender about buying discount points. This involves paying an upfront fee to reduce your interest rate, saving you thousands over the life of the loan.
- Consider a 15-year mortgage instead of a 30-year mortgage if you can afford the higher payments. This will save you significant interest over time.

3. Prepare for Unexpected Repairs:

- Set aside 1–2% of your home's value annually for maintenance and repairs. For example, if your home is worth $200,000, aim to save $2,000 to $4,000 per year.

- Invest in a home warranty, especially during the first year, to cover major systems like HVAC or plumbing.

4. Pay Off Your Mortgage Faster:

- Make biweekly payments instead of monthly payments. This results in one extra payment per year, reducing your principal faster.
- Use windfalls (e.g., tax refunds, bonuses) to make additional payments toward the principal.
- Refinance to a shorter loan term if it aligns with your financial goals.

Additional Smart Financial Advice

1. Build an Emergency Fund: Unexpected expenses happen, and having a safety net prevents you from relying on credit cards. Aim to save 3–6 months of living expenses.
2. Avoid Impulse Purchases: Before buying something, ask yourself if it's a want or a

Increasing Income and Making Smart Choices

need. Give yourself 24 hours to think it over.
3. Invest in Yourself: Whether it's learning a new skill, furthering your education, or improving your health, investing in yourself can pay off financially and personally.
4. Plan for the Future: Save for retirement as early as possible. Even small contributions grow over time thanks to compound interest.

Smart financial decisions don't have to be perfect, but they should reflect your goals and values. By taking the time to plan, research, and make thoughtful choices, you can avoid unnecessary debt and create a stable foundation for the future.

SECTION 4

NAVIGATING COMPLEX FINANCIAL CHALLENGES

Chapter 11

Handling Medical Debt

Medical debt is one of the most overwhelming types of debt, often arising unexpectedly. A single medical emergency or procedure can lead to thousands of dollars in bills, leaving you stressed and unsure of what to do next. However, there are practical ways to manage medical debt effectively and prevent it from derailing your financial progress.

Steps to Manage Medical Debt

1. Review Your Bills Thoroughly

- Always request an itemized bill. Medical bills often contain errors, such as duplicate charges or incorrect procedures. Carefully review each line item to ensure accuracy.
- If you spot an error, contact your provider immediately to have it corrected. This simple step can significantly reduce your total cost.

2. Understand Your Insurance

- Review your insurance policy to see what's covered and confirm your responsibility.
- If a claim is denied, don't accept it at face value. Contact your insurance company, provide documentation, and file an appeal if necessary.

3. Negotiate with Providers

- Many hospitals, clinics, and dental offices are willing to negotiate the cost of services. Ask if they offer discounts for paying upfront or reduced rates for patients without insurance.
- Some providers will also reduce your bill if you can demonstrate financial hardship.

Navigating Complex Financial Challenges

4. Ask About Financial Assistance Programs

- ♦ Hospitals are required to provide financial assistance programs for eligible patients. Inquire about these options, as they can drastically reduce or even eliminate your bill.
- ♦ Submit the necessary paperwork to determine if you qualify. Many people are unaware of these programs and miss out on significant savings.

5. Set Up a 0% Interest Payment Plan

- ♦ Instead of transferring your medical debt to a high-interest credit card, work with your provider to create an interest-free payment plan. Most hospitals and dental offices are willing to work with you to create a manageable monthly payment schedule.

6. Always Get Agreements in Writing

- ♦ Before making payments, ensure that any negotiated discounts, payment plans, or financial assistance agreements are documented in writing. This protects you if disputes arise later.

7. Request a Paid-in-Full Letter

   ♦ Once you've completed payments, ask for a paid-in-full letter from the provider. Keep this document for your records in case the debt is mistakenly sent to collections in the future.

Personal Story

After an unexpected medical emergency, I received a bill for $1,800 that I couldn't pay upfront. The first thing I did was call the hospital and explain my situation. The billing department was surprisingly helpful—they offered to reduce the bill by 20% if I paid a portion upfront, and the remaining balance was set up on a 0% interest payment plan.

I also requested an itemized bill and noticed a duplicate charge for a procedure. Once I pointed it out, they corrected the error, which reduced my total even further.

Staying proactive and communicating with the billing department not only saved me money but also reduced my stress. Medical debt can feel overwhelming, but there are solutions if you're willing to advocate for yourself.

Tips for Navigating Medical Debt

- Ask About Discounts:Many providers offer discounts if you pay upfront or within a specific timeframe.
- Explore Assistance Programs: Check if you qualify for financial aid through your hospital, local programs, or nonprofit organizations.
- Request an Itemized Bill: Always verify your charges to avoid paying for errors or duplicate entries.
- Be Persistent: If an insurance claim is denied, appeal the decision. Provide documentation and follow up regularly.
- Document Everything: Keep records of all communication with providers and insurance companies.

Activity: Create a Medical Debt Plan

Use the following table to organize and track your medical debts. Include details like the provider, balance, payment terms, and monthly payment amount:

Provider	Balance	Payment Plan	Monthly Payment
City Hospital	$1,800	Interest-Free Plan	$100
Dental Clinic	$500	Lump-Sum Discount	$400
Specialist Office	$1,200	Negotiated Payment	$50

At the end of each month, revisit this table to track your progress. Adjust your plan as needed, and don't hesitate to contact providers if your financial situation changes.

Handling medical debt can feel like an uphill battle, but with these steps and strategies, you can manage it effectively and prevent it from spiraling out of control. Be proactive, stay persistent, and don't be afraid to ask for help—your financial health depends on it.

Chapter 12

Creative Ways to Cut Costs

Why It's Important

Cutting costs doesn't mean depriving yourself of the things you love. It's about being resourceful, intentional, and finding innovative ways to save money while still enjoying life. Every dollar saved can be redirected toward paying off debt, building an emergency fund, or achieving other financial goals.

This chapter offers practical and creative strategies to reduce expenses without sacrificing your quality of life.

Frugal Hacks for Everyday Life

1. Meal Prep for Savings and Convenience

Meal prepping is a game-changer for saving money on food. By planning and preparing meals in advance, you'll reduce waste, avoid costly takeout, and have healthier options ready to go.

- ♦ Practical Tip: Plan your meals for the week, shop with a list, and cook in bulk. For example, roast a whole chicken to use in salads, soups, and sandwiches throughout the week.

2. DIY Home Solutions

Take on simple home repairs and projects yourself to save on labor costs. YouTube tutorials are excellent resources for learning how to fix leaky faucets, paint walls, or assemble furniture.

- ♦ Practical Tip: Invest in a basic toolbox and a few quality tools for common household fixes.

3. Maximize Cashback and Rewards Programs

Use cashback apps like Rakuten, Ibotta, or Fetch Rewards to earn money on purchases you're already making.

- Practical Tip: Stack cashback offers with coupons and sales to maximize savings.

4. Save on Transportation Costs

- Use public transportation, carpool, or bike whenever possible.
- Shop around for the best auto insurance rates every six months to ensure you're getting the best deal.

Bartering and Trading Services

Why It Works:

Bartering is a win-win way to save money by exchanging skills or items you no longer need.

Examples:

- Offer babysitting services in exchange for help with yard work.
- Trade professional skills (e.g., graphic design, writing) for services like house cleaning or car repairs.
- Join online bartering communities or local Facebook groups to find opportunities.

Secondhand Shopping

Why It's Smart:

Shopping secondhand saves money and is eco-friendly. Many thrift stores, consignment shops, and online marketplaces offer quality items at a fraction of the cost.

What to Look For:

- Furniture, home decor, and appliances.
- Gently used clothing, especially for kids who outgrow items quickly.
- Sports equipment, books, and toys.

Practical Tip:

Set alerts on platforms like Facebook Marketplace or Craigslist to snag deals on specific items you're looking for.

Couponing and BOGO Deals

Coupons and "buy one, get one" (BOGO) deals are simple yet effective ways to save on everyday purchases.

Practical Tips:
1. Digital Coupons: Use store apps to access digital coupons for groceries, household items, and more.

2. Manufacturer Coupons: Look for coupons on product websites or inside packaging.
3. Double Up Savings: Combine coupons with store sales to maximize discounts.
4. BOGO Deals: Stock up on non-perishables during BOGO sales to stretch your dollar further.

Entertainment on a Budget

Having fun doesn't have to cost a fortune. Here are creative ways to enjoy entertainment for less:

- Free Events: Look for free concerts, festivals, or museum days in your community.
- Streaming Savings: Share streaming subscriptions with family or friends.
- Host Game Nights: Invite friends over for board games or card games instead of going out.
- DIY Date Nights: Have a picnic in the park, stargaze, or cook a special meal together at home.

Utilities and Household Expenses

Reducing utility costs is one of the easiest ways to save money. Small changes can add up over time:

- Switch to Energy-Efficient Bulbs: LED bulbs use less energy and last longer.
- Unplug Devices: Electronics draw power even when not in use.
- Lower Your Thermostat: Adjusting your thermostat by a few degrees can save on heating and cooling costs.

Creative Money Challenges

1. The "No-Spend" Challenge:

Commit to spending money only on essentials for a set period (e.g., a week or a month). Use the savings to pay down debt or boost your emergency fund.

2. The 52-Week Savings Challenge:

Save $1 in the first week, $2 in the second week, and so on. By the end of the year, you'll have saved $1,378.

3. The Pantry Challenge:

For one week, avoid grocery shopping and focus on using up items you already have in your pantry and freezer.

Unexpected Savings Opportunities

1. Negotiate Your Bills

- Call service providers (e.g., cable, internet, or phone companies) and ask for discounts or promotions. Be polite but firm, and mention competitors' offers if needed.

2. Take Advantage of Tax-Free Holidays

- Many states offer tax-free weekends for back-to-school shopping or energy-efficient appliances. Plan your purchases around these events to save.

3. Switch to Generic Brands

- Store-brand products are often just as good as name brands but cost significantly less.

Making Small Changes for Big Savings

Small, consistent changes in your daily habits can lead to significant savings over time:

- Brew your coffee at home instead of visiting coffee shops.
- Pack your lunch instead of eating out.
- Repair clothes or shoes instead of replacing them.

Activity: Identify Your Top 3 Cost-Saving Opportunities

Take a few minutes to reflect on your spending habits and where you can cut costs. Use the table below to list your top opportunities:

Expense Category	Current Spending	Potential Savings
Groceries		
Entertainment		
Utilities		

Total Savings Potential: $_____/month (or $_____/year!)

Final Thoughts

Cutting costs doesn't mean you have to give up everything you enjoy. It's about finding creative ways to live well while spending less. By implementing even a few of these strategies, you can free up money to pay down debt, save for emergencies, or work toward your financial goals.

Every dollar saved is a step closer to financial freedom. Small changes lead to big results over time—start today, and watch the impact grow.

Section 5

Maintaining Financial Freedom

Chapter 13

Staying Debt-Free

Paying off your debt is a monumental achievement, but staying debt-free is an ongoing journey that requires consistent effort and vigilance. It's easy to slip back into old habits, but with the right mindset and strategies, you can maintain your hard-earned success and continue building a life of stability, freedom, and joy.

Staying debt-free isn't just about money—it's about improving your overall quality of life. From financial security to better mental and physical health, the benefits of staying out of debt are transformative and far-reaching.

Why Staying Debt-Free Matters

Becoming debt-free isn't just about eliminating balances—it's about changing your relationship with money. Debt often brings stress, anxiety, and limitations, while financial freedom opens doors to opportunities and peace of mind. Staying debt-free allows you to focus on your goals, build wealth, and enjoy life without the constant burden of payments hanging over your head.

The Benefits of Staying Debt-Free

1. Financial Benefits

- ♦ More Disposable Income: With no debt payments, your money is yours to save, invest, or spend on things that truly matter to you.
- ♦ Ability to Build Wealth: Staying debt-free allows you to focus on saving for retirement, investing, or building an emergency fund.
- ♦ Increased Financial Security: Without debt, you're better prepared for unexpected expenses or economic downturns.
- ♦ Improved Credit Score: By maintaining good financial habits, you can improve your

credit score, giving you access to better interest rates if you ever need a loan.

2. Emotional Benefits

- ♦ Peace of Mind: The relief of knowing you don't owe money to anyone is priceless.
- ♦ Confidence and Empowerment: Staying debt-free reinforces your ability to manage money and make smart financial decisions.
- ♦ Reduced Anxiety: Financial struggles often lead to stress and worry. Eliminating debt removes one of the biggest sources of anxiety for many people.

3. Physical and Mental Health Benefits

- ♦ Lower Stress Levels: Financial stress takes a toll on your physical and mental health. Staying debt-free reduces stress, improving your overall well-being.
- ♦ Better Sleep: Without the weight of debt on your mind, you're likely to sleep better at night.
- ♦ More Energy: Financial freedom allows you to focus on self-care and pursue activities that bring you joy and vitality.

4. Relationship Benefits

- Improved Communication: Couples often argue about money. Being debt-free allows you and your partner to have more productive and positive financial discussions.
- Freedom to Support Loved Ones: Without debt, you can provide financial help to family members or invest in meaningful experiences together.
- Stronger Partnerships: Debt-free living fosters trust and teamwork in relationships as you work together toward shared goals.

Strategies for Staying Debt-Free

Here are some practical steps to ensure you stay on track:

1. Build an Emergency Fund

- Save 3–6 months of living expenses to cover unexpected costs without relying on credit cards.
- Pro Tip: Automate your savings by setting up direct transfers to a high-yield savings account.

Personal Insight:

After COVID-19, I firmly believe everyone should aim for at least a six-month emergency fund. During the pandemic, unemployment took a long time for many people to process. If you didn't qualify for unemployment, you were left with no safety net. Having an emergency fund can make all the difference in times of uncertainty.

2. Continue Budgeting

- Treat budgeting as a lifelong habit. Regularly track your income and expenses to stay in control of your finances.

3. Set Financial Goals

- Whether it's saving for a home, retirement, or a dream vacation, having clear goals will keep you motivated and focused.

4. Avoid Lifestyle Inflation

- As your income increases, resist the temptation to upgrade your lifestyle unnecessarily. Instead, allocate extra funds toward savings, investments, or paying down your mortgage.

5. Pay Off Credit Cards in Full
    - Use credit cards responsibly and pay off the balance in full every month to avoid interest charges.

6. Compare Credit vs. Cash
    - Using Credit Cards: Great for building credit, earning rewards, and handling emergencies, but only if you're disciplined.
    - Using Cash: Helps control spending, as studies show people spend less when using cash.

7. Automate Your Savings
    - Set up automatic transfers to your savings, investment accounts, or retirement fund.

8. Review Your Financial Plan Regularly
    - Life circumstances change—whether it's a new job, a baby, or a move. Revisit your financial plan annually to make adjustments and stay aligned with your goals.

9. Stay Educated
    - Personal finance is always evolving. Read books, listen to podcasts, or take online courses to stay informed about managing money effectively.

10. Celebrate Milestones Mindfully
- ♦ Reward yourself when you hit financial goals, but do so within your budget. For example, treat yourself to a dinner out, a small splurge, or a meaningful experience that won't derail your progress.

Personal Story: The Day I Became Debt-Free

I remember the exact day I became debt-free. It was one of the most relieving and empowering feelings I've ever experienced. Knowing that my paychecks no longer had to go toward credit cards, medical bills, or other debts felt like a huge weight had been lifted.

At first, I was terrified to touch my credit cards again. I kept one card in my wallet for emergencies and locked the others away. Instead, I relied heavily on cash. I would withdraw $100 from the ATM, and that became my budget for whatever I needed.

Using cash taught me discipline. It's true—statistics show that people spend less when they use cash instead of credit cards. When you physically see the money leaving your hand, you think twice about spending it. Over time, I regained confidence in my ability to manage credit cards responsibly and began using them strategically for rewards while paying them off in full each month.

Maintaining Financial Freedom

Final Thoughts

Staying debt-free isn't just about the numbers—it's about creating a life of freedom, stability, and joy. Financial freedom allows you to focus on what truly matters, whether it's building your dream home, traveling the world, or simply enjoying peace of mind.

The benefits of staying debt-free ripple through every aspect of your life. From improved relationships and reduced stress to better sleep and a stronger sense of empowerment, the rewards are immeasurable. You've already proven you can take control of your finances. Now, it's about staying consistent and making intentional decisions to protect your financial future.

You've got this!

Chapter 14

The Psychology of Debt-Free Living

Why It's Important

Paying off debt is more than a financial accomplishment—it's a mental and emotional transformation. The psychology behind debt-free living involves understanding your beliefs, habits, and mindset about money. Without addressing these deeper issues, it's easy to fall back into old patterns that lead to debt. Shifting your mindset to prioritize financial freedom and cultivating healthy habits are critical steps to achieving and maintaining a debt-free lifestyle.

Breaking Free from the Debt Mindset

Debt often creates a sense of scarcity and limitation. The feeling of "not having enough" can lead to stress, shame, and even hopelessness. To break free, it's essential to identify and challenge the negative beliefs that keep you stuck.

Common Limiting Beliefs About Money:

1. "I'll always be in debt."

   - Reality: With the right plan and discipline, anyone can become debt-free.

2. "I deserve to treat myself."

   - Reality: Self-care doesn't have to mean overspending; it's about balance.

3. "Debt is just a part of life."

   - Reality: Debt may be common, but it's not inevitable. Financial freedom is achievable with intention and effort.

The Emotional Toll of Debt

Debt isn't just a financial burden—it's an emotional one. It can lead to feelings of failure, stress, and even depression. Recognizing the emotional toll is the first step to reclaiming your power.

Signs of the Emotional Impact of Debt:

- Avoiding mail or phone calls for fear of collection notices.
- Constantly worrying about money, even in non-financial situations.
- Feeling guilty or ashamed about past financial decisions.

Practical Tip:

Write down how debt makes you feel. Then, write how being debt-free will make you feel. Use these reflections to motivate yourself during difficult times.

Mindset Shifts for Debt-Free Living

1. Let Go of Comparison

Comparing your financial journey to others can be discouraging and unproductive. Social media often highlights the best moments in others' lives but rarely shows their struggles.

Affirmation: "I am focused on my own goals and progress, not someone else's timeline."

2. Focus on Abundance, Not Scarcity

A scarcity mindset—feeling like there's never enough—can lead to hoarding money or overspending out of fear. Shift to an abundance mindset by celebrating small wins and trusting in your ability to create opportunities.

Practical Tip:

List three things you're grateful for each day, focusing on what you already have instead of what you lack.

3. Reframe Setbacks as Learning Opportunities

Mistakes are inevitable, but they're also valuable lessons. Instead of dwelling on financial missteps, analyze what went wrong and how to avoid similar situations in the future.

Example:

If you overspend one month, identify the trigger (e.g., emotional spending, poor planning) and create a strategy to prevent it next time.

Building Healthy Money Habits

1. Develop a Growth Mindset:

A growth mindset is the belief that you can improve through effort and learning. Apply this to your finances by seeing each step—no matter how small—as progress.

2. Practice Delayed Gratification:

One of the most powerful habits for staying debt-free is delaying gratification. Instead of making impulsive purchases, save for what you want and enjoy the process of working toward your goals.

Practical Tip:

Before making a non-essential purchase, wait 24 hours. If you still want it after the waiting period, ensure it fits within your budget.

3. Automate Good Financial Habits:

- Set up automatic bill payments to avoid late fees.
- Automate savings so you're consistently building a financial cushion.

The Rewards of Debt-Free Living

Debt-free living isn't just about financial freedom—it's about emotional and mental freedom as well. Here's how it impacts every aspect of your life:

1. Financial Freedom:

- You can focus on saving, investing, and spending on things that truly matter to you.

2. Emotional Relief:

    ♦ Say goodbye to the stress and anxiety that debt brings. Enjoy the peace of knowing you owe nothing to anyone.

3. Improved Relationships:

    ♦ Money is one of the leading causes of stress in relationships. Being debt-free fosters open communication and trust.

4. Personal Empowerment:

    ♦ Achieving a debt-free life proves that you're capable of overcoming challenges and creating the future you want.

Maintaining Financial Freedom

Activity: Redefine Your Money Mindset

1. Reflect on Your Beliefs About Money:

    ♦ What messages about money did you hear growing up?
    ♦ How do those messages influence your spending and saving habits today?

2. Set New Intentions:

    ♦ Write a money mantra that reflects your financial goals. Example: "I am financially disciplined and create opportunities for abundance."

3. Create a Vision Board:

    ♦ Use images, words, or quotes that represent your debt-free life. Display it where you'll see it daily as a source of motivation.

Final Thoughts

The journey to becoming and staying debt-free starts with your mindset. By understanding your relationship with money and shifting your perspective, you can transform your financial habits and create lasting change.

Remember: You are not defined by your debt. With patience, persistence, and a positive outlook, you can achieve financial freedom and live a life of abundance and stability.

CHAPTER 15

How to Say No and Set Boundaries

Why It's Important

One of the most challenging aspects of achieving financial freedom is managing the social and emotional pressures that come with saying "no." Whether it's declining a night out with friends, skipping a big family vacation, or setting financial boundaries with loved ones, saying no can feel uncomfortable. However, it's a critical skill for staying on track with your financial goals.

Setting boundaries isn't about denying yourself or others; it's about protecting your priorities and ensuring your choices align with your values and financial goals. This chapter will help you learn how to say no gracefully, establish healthy financial boundaries, and maintain relationships while staying true to your goals.

The Emotional Challenges of Saying No

Saying no can feel awkward, especially when you're worried about disappointing others or being perceived as stingy. These emotional hurdles often lead people to say yes to things they can't afford, setting them back financially.

Common Challenges:

1. Guilt: Feeling like you're letting someone down by declining their request.
2. Fear of Missing Out (FOMO): Worrying that you'll miss out on experiences or opportunities.
3. Peer Pressure: Feeling obligated to keep up with others' lifestyles or spending habits.

Reframing Your Mindset:

- ♦ Remember that saying no to one thing means saying yes to something else—your goals, peace of mind, and financial freedom.

Maintaining Financial Freedom

- Understand that true friends and family will respect your boundaries when you communicate with them honestly.

How to Say No Gracefully

1. Be Honest, Not Defensive

You don't have to justify your decision with a detailed explanation. A simple, polite response is enough.

- Example: "Thank you for inviting me, but I'm focusing on my budget right now."

2. Offer Alternatives

Suggest cost-effective alternatives that allow you to participate without compromising your financial goals.

- Example: "I can't join for dinner, but I'd love to meet for coffee instead."

3. Use Humor to Diffuse Awkwardness

Sometimes a lighthearted response can ease the tension.

- Example: "I'd love to go, but my wallet says otherwise!"

4. Delay Your Response if Needed

If you're unsure how to respond, give yourself time to think.

- ♦ Example: "Let me check my schedule and get back to you."

Setting Financial Boundaries with Loved Ones

Setting boundaries with family and friends can be particularly challenging, especially if they're used to you saying yes. Here's how to navigate these situations:

1. Communicate Your Goals Clearly

Share your financial goals with loved ones so they understand why you're setting boundaries.

- ♦ Example: "I'm working on paying off my debt, so I need to cut back on expenses for a while."

2. Set Limits on Lending Money

It's okay to help loved ones in need, but it's equally important to protect your financial health.

- ♦ Practical Tip: Only lend money if you can afford to lose it and set clear repayment terms upfront.

3. Establish Spending Limits for Group Activities

When planning group activities, suggest affordable options that everyone can enjoy.

- ♦ Example: "Instead of going out to dinner, why don't we do a potluck at my place?"

4. Learn to Say No to Family Obligations

Cultural or familial expectations can sometimes pressure you to overspend. It's okay to politely decline or contribute in a way that aligns with your budget.

- ♦ Example: "I can't contribute as much as I'd like, but I'd love to help in other ways."

Recognizing and Avoiding Lifestyle Creep

As you earn more money, it's tempting to upgrade your lifestyle. This phenomenon, known as lifestyle creep, can sabotage your financial progress.

Tips to Avoid Lifestyle Creep:

1. Automate Savings: Direct a portion of any pay raise or bonus into savings or investments before you can spend it.
2. Stick to Your Budget: Treat increases in income as opportunities to save more, not spend more.

3. Practice Gratitude: Focus on the things you already have rather than what you think you need.

Overcoming the Fear of Missing Out (FOMO)

FOMO is a powerful driver of overspending. Social media often fuels this feeling by showing us the highlights of other people's lives.

How to Manage FOMO:
1. Limit Social Media Exposure: Take breaks from social platforms that make you feel pressured to keep up with others.
2. Focus on Your Goals: Remind yourself why you're making financial sacrifices. Visualize the long-term rewards of your decisions.
3. Create Your Own Joy: Find free or low-cost activities that bring you happiness, such as hiking, reading, or spending time with loved ones.

Building Confidence in Your Decisions

The more you practice saying no and setting boundaries, the more confident you'll become in prioritizing your financial goals.

Maintaining Financial Freedom

Tips for Building Confidence:

1. Celebrate Small Wins: Each time you successfully stick to your budget or decline an expense, acknowledge your progress.
2. Use Affirmations: Repeat empowering statements like, "I am in control of my finances," or "I prioritize my future over temporary pleasures."
3. Lean on Your Support System: Surround yourself with people who encourage and respect your financial journey.

Activity: Practice Saying No

Here are some common scenarios where you might need to say no, along with examples of how to respond gracefully. Use these as inspiration to craft your own responses:

1. A Friend Invites You to an Expensive Dinner

    ♦ "Thanks for inviting me! I'm trying to stick to my budget right now, but I'd love to catch up over coffee instead."
    ♦ "I can't make it this time, but let's plan something more low-key soon."

2. A Family Member Asks to Borrow Money

    ♦ "I'm sorry, I can't lend money right now, but I'm here to support you in other ways."
    ♦ "I'd love to help, but I'm focused on my financial goals and can't take on extra expenses at the moment."

3. Coworkers Suggest a Pricey Happy Hour

    ♦ "That sounds like fun, but I'm cutting back on expenses. Let me know if you want to plan something less expensive next time!"
    ♦ "I'm skipping happy hour this week, but I'll join you for lunch in the breakroom tomorrow!"

4. A Group Plans an Expensive Vacation or Event

- "That trip sounds amazing, but it's not in my budget right now. I'll be cheering you on from home!"
- "I can't swing the cost this year, but let's plan something smaller for the group later."

5. A Partner or Spouse Wants to Make a Big Purchase

- "I think that's a great idea, but let's save up for it first so we don't have to use credit."
- "Let's revisit this once we've made progress on our financial goals."

6. Your Child Asks for Something Outside the Budget

- "That's a cool toy, but it's not in the budget right now. Let's add it to your wishlist for a future treat."
- "I know you want this, but we're saving for something even more exciting. Let's work toward that goal together!"

7. Friends Expect You to Split a Big Bill Equally

- "I'd prefer to pay for what I ordered since I'm watching my budget. I hope that's okay with everyone."

- "I'll cover my share, but I'll skip the extras this time."

8. A Family Member Expects You to Contribute More Financially

- "I understand this is important, but I need to be mindful of my financial limits. I can contribute what I can afford, and I hope that helps."
- "I wish I could give more, but this is all I can do right now."

Pro Tip: Practice these responses out loud or write them down. The more comfortable you are with your words, the easier it will be to stay firm and confident when the moment arises.

Final Thoughts

Saying no and setting financial boundaries isn't about being selfish—it's about prioritizing your well-being and goals. By learning how to decline gracefully and communicate your boundaries effectively, you can maintain healthy relationships while staying true to your financial journey.

Remember, every time you say no to something that doesn't align with your goals, you're saying yes to your future. With practice and confidence, you'll find that setting boundaries becomes second nature—and your finances will thank you for it.

Chapter 16

Financial Planning for Families

Why It's Important

Managing family finances is a balancing act. From ensuring your family's needs are met today to planning for future expenses, financial stability is key to providing security and peace of mind. Thoughtful financial planning helps families navigate day-to-day expenses, prepare for emergencies, and build wealth for future generations.

This chapter will guide you through practical steps to manage your family's finances, from budgeting to estate planning, ensuring your loved ones are protected and prepared for the future.

Budgeting for Families

Why Budgeting Matters:

A family budget ensures that your financial priorities are in order. With multiple people depending on your income, it's crucial to track every dollar and allocate resources effectively.

Steps to Create a Family Budget:

1. Track Income and Expenses: Include all sources of income and regular expenses like groceries, childcare, and transportation.
2. Separate Needs from Wants: Prioritize essential expenses (e.g., rent, utilities) over discretionary spending (e.g., entertainment).
3. Involve the Entire Family: Teach kids about budgeting by explaining how money is allocated and encouraging them to participate in saving goals.
4. Plan for Unexpected Costs: Set aside a portion of your budget for emergencies, such as medical expenses or car repairs.

Pro Tip:

Batch-cook meals to save money and time. For example, cook a large pot of pasta or soup that can last several meals. This reduces dining-out expenses and minimizes food waste.

Teaching Kids About Money

Why It's Important:

Teaching your children about money helps them develop good financial habits early. This not only benefits them but also creates a more financially conscious household.

Age-Appropriate Money Lessons:

1. Toddlers and Preschoolers:
- ♦ Teach them about saving and spending using a piggy bank.

2. Elementary School Kids:
- ♦ Introduce concepts like earning money through chores and dividing it into spending, saving, and giving categories.

3. Teens:
- ♦ Encourage part-time jobs and guide them in opening a savings account to learn financial independence.

Practical Tip:

If you own a business, hire your children to help with age-appropriate tasks. Not only do they gain valuable work experience, but their income may be tax-deductible for your business. In 2023, children earning under $13,850 typically do not pay federal income taxes (check current laws).

Saving for Your Children's Future

Planning for your children's future expenses—like college or starting their own lives—is an important part of financial planning.

1. High-Yield Savings Accounts

High-yield savings accounts (HYSAs) are an excellent way to save for your child's future while earning interest.

Pros:

- Flexible: Funds can be used for any purpose (e.g., college, a car, or a wedding).
- Accessible: Easy to deposit and withdraw funds without penalties.
- Low Risk: Savings accounts are insured and stable.

Cons:

- Lower Returns: Interest rates are lower compared to investment options.
- Inflation Risk: The value of the savings may decrease over time due to inflation.

Practical Tip:

Open a HYSA for your child and set up automated deposits. Even $25 a month can grow significantly over time.

2. 529 College Savings Plan

A 529 plan is a tax-advantaged savings account specifically designed for education expenses.

Pros:

- Tax Benefits: Earnings grow tax-free if used for qualified education expenses.
- High Contribution Limits: Allows significant savings for college or K-12 tuition.

Cons:

- Restricted Use: Funds must be used for education-related expenses, or you'll face penalties.
- Market Risk: Investments can lose value depending on market performance.

My Take:

If you're unsure whether your child will need the funds for education, a high-yield savings account or other flexible savings options may be a better choice.

Estate Planning for Families

Estate planning is critical for protecting your family's assets and ensuring your wishes are honored after your passing. It's not just for the wealthy—every family benefits from having clear plans in place.

1. The Importance of a Will and Testament

A will ensures that your assets are distributed according to your wishes and protects your loved ones from legal disputes.

Why You Need a Will:

- Designate guardians for minor children.
- Specify how your assets, including money, property, and personal belongings, should be distributed.
- Avoid confusion and reduce the burden on your family during a difficult time.

Practical Tip:

Work with an estate planning attorney to draft a legally binding will. Keep it updated as your circumstances change, such as the birth of a child or the purchase of a home.

2. Beneficiary Designations

Many financial accounts, such as life insurance policies, retirement accounts, and savings accounts, allow you to name a beneficiary.

Why It's Important:

- ♦ Ensures that funds are distributed directly to the intended person without going through probate.
- ♦ Simplifies the process for your family and ensures faster access to funds.

Practical Tip:

Review and update beneficiary designations regularly, especially after major life events like marriage, divorce, or the birth of a child.

3. Trusts for Major Assets

A trust can protect your home or other significant assets and provide for your family in a more controlled way than a will.

Benefits of a Trust:

- ♦ Avoids probate, ensuring a faster and more private transfer of assets.
- ♦ Allows you to set conditions for how and when assets are distributed (e.g., your child receives funds only after turning 21).
- ♦ Protects assets from creditors or lawsuits.

Practical Tip:

If you own a home or significant assets, consider setting up a trust to ensure your family's long-term financial security.

Tax Strategies for Families

1. Claim Tax Credits:

- ♦ Take advantage of family-focused tax credits, such as the Child Tax Credit or Dependent Care Credit, to lower your tax liability.

2. Maximize Deductions:

- ♦ Deduct eligible expenses, such as childcare, medical costs, or educational expenses, to reduce taxable income.

Maintaining Financial Freedom

3. Leverage Business Deductions:
- If your child works for your family business, their wages may be tax-deductible. Ensure their income stays within limits to avoid federal taxes.

Final Thoughts

Financial planning for families is about more than managing money—it's about creating security, stability, and opportunities for your loved ones. By budgeting, saving, and planning for the future, you can build a strong financial foundation that supports your family's dreams and protects them from uncertainty.

Every step you take—no matter how small—brings you closer to a financially secure future for your family. Start today, and set the example for the next generation.

Chapter 17

Investing While Paying Off Debt

Why It's Important

For many people, the idea of investing while paying off debt seems counterintuitive. After all, why put money into investments when you owe money elsewhere? However, in some situations, investing can be a smart financial move—even while tackling debt. The key is to balance these two priorities wisely. This chapter will guide you through the pros and cons of investing while in debt, practical strategies, and trusted tools to help you make informed decisions.

The Pros of Investing While Paying Off Debt

1. Compounding Growth:

Investing early allows your money to grow exponentially over time thanks to compound interest. The earlier you start, the more time your investments have to multiply.

2. Taking Advantage of Employer Benefits:

Many employers offer retirement plans, like a 401(k), with matching contributions. This is essentially free money, so not contributing means leaving money on the table.

3. Diversifying Financial Goals:

Paying off debt is essential, but investing allows you to build wealth simultaneously, preparing for long-term goals like retirement or homeownership.

4. Inflation Protection:

Money sitting in a standard savings account often loses value over time due to inflation. Investments, on the other hand, have the potential to outpace inflation.

The Cons of Investing While Paying Off Debt

1. High-Interest Debt May Offset Gains:

If you're carrying high-interest debt, such as credit card debt with a 20% APR, it's likely more beneficial to focus on paying it off before investing. Most investments won't yield returns higher than the interest you're paying.

2. Split Focus:

Trying to tackle both investing and debt repayment can dilute your efforts, making it harder to achieve either goal quickly.

3. Market Risk:

Unlike paying off debt, which offers guaranteed returns (you save on interest payments), investing comes with risks. Markets fluctuate, and there's no guarantee you'll make money in the short term.

When to Prioritize Investing Over Debt Repayment

1. Low-Interest Debt:

If your debt has a low interest rate (e.g., under 5%), investing may offer better long-term returns. For example, historical stock market returns average around 7–10% annually.

2. Employer-Matched Retirement Plans:

Always contribute enough to your 401(k) or similar plan to take full advantage of employer matching. This is essentially a 100% return on your contributions.

3. Building an Emergency Fund First:

Before prioritizing investments, ensure you have an emergency fund with at least three months of living expenses. This safety net prevents you from relying on credit cards during unexpected situations.

When to Focus Solely on Debt Repayment

1. High-Interest Debt:

Debt with an interest rate higher than 8–10% should be paid off as quickly as possible, as it likely outweighs potential investment returns.

2. Unstable Financial Situation:

If you're struggling to make ends meet or lack an emergency fund, prioritize paying off debt and stabilizing your finances before investing.

Practical Tips for Investing While Paying Off Debt

1. Start Small:

You don't need to invest thousands to get started. Begin with as little as $10 a week using micro-investing apps.

2. Balance Priorities:

Allocate a percentage of your budget to both goals. For example, put 80% toward debt repayment and 20% toward investments. Adjust as your financial situation improves.

3. Use Tax-Advantaged Accounts:

Contribute to retirement accounts like a 401(k) or IRA to take advantage of tax benefits. These accounts reduce taxable income and allow your money to grow tax-free.

4. Diversify Investments:

Don't put all your money into one stock or asset. Use low-cost index funds or exchange-traded funds (ETFs) to spread risk across multiple investments.

Trusted Investment Platforms and Apps

Here are some reputable companies and apps to help you start investing:

1. Fidelity Investments:

   ♦ Known for low-cost index funds, excellent customer service, and comprehensive tools for beginners and advanced investors.
   ♦ Offers retirement accounts (e.g., IRAs) and taxable brokerage accounts.

2. Vanguard:

   ♦ A leader in low-cost index funds and ETFs. Ideal for long-term investors focused on retirement savings.

3. Charles Schwab:

   ♦ Offers robust investment tools, commission-free trades, and educational resources for new investors.

4. Acorns:

   ♦ A micro-investing app that rounds up your purchases and invests the spare change. Perfect for beginners who want to start small.

5. Robinhood:
- ◆ Commission-free trading with a user-friendly app. Best for those looking to invest in individual stocks or ETFs.

6. Betterment:
- ◆ A robo-advisor that builds and manages a diversified portfolio for you. It's an excellent option for hands-off investors.

7. M1 Finance:
- ◆ Combines automation with customization, allowing you to create your own investment portfolio or use pre-designed templates.

Long-Term Investing Strategies

1. Focus on the Long Game:
- ◆ Avoid getting caught up in daily market fluctuations. Investing is about building wealth over decades, not days.

2. Automate Contributions:
- ◆ Set up automatic transfers to your investment account to stay consistent, even when life gets busy.

3. Reinvest Dividends:
   - Opt to reinvest dividends from stocks or funds to maximize growth through compounding.

4. Educate Yourself:
   - Continuously learn about investing by reading books, attending webinars, or following trusted financial advisors online.

Activity: Create an Investment Plan

Use this table to outline your current debt, investment goals, and action plan:

Category	Details
Debt Interest Rate	High-interest (10%) or low-interest (4%)?
Investment Goal	Retirement, emergency fund, or wealth building?
Budget Allocation	% to debt repayment vs. investments
Next Step	Open an account, automate contributions, etc.

Final Thoughts

Investing while paying off debt is a balancing act that requires careful planning and discipline. Start by evaluating your financial situation, prioritizing high-interest debt repayment, and taking advantage of opportunities like employer-matched retirement plans.

Even small investments can grow significantly over time, so don't underestimate the power of starting small. By balancing debt repayment and investing wisely, you can secure your financial future while achieving freedom from debt.

Remember: Every dollar invested today is a step toward building a stable, abundant tomorrow.

Section 6

Closing Inspiration

Worksheets

The following worksheets are designed to help you organize your finances, track your progress, and stay motivated on your journey to becoming debt-free. Feel free to print and use these templates as often as needed.

These tools are essential for visualizing your progress, maintaining accountability, and staying motivated throughout your debt-free journey.

DEBT TRACKING WORKSHEET

Use this worksheet to record all your debts, including creditors, balances, interest rates, and minimum payments. Revisit this table at the end of each month to update your progress and stay on track.

Example:

Debt Type	Creditor	Balance	Interest Rate	Minimum Payment

Monthly Budget Template

This worksheet helps you track your income and expenses. Allocate your spending to necessary categories and compare planned amounts with actual amounts each month to identify areas for improvement.

Example:

Account	Planned Amount	Actual Account
Rent/ Mortgage		
Utilities		
Groceries		
Transportation		
Debt Payments		
Savings		
Fun/ Entertainment		

Debt Snowball Tracker

The Debt Snowball Method focuses on paying off smaller debts first to build momentum. Use this tracker to organize your debts in payoff order and monitor your progress.

Example:

Creditor/Account	Due Date	Minimum Payment	Interest Rate	Total Balance
Rent/Mortgage				

Savings Goal Chart

This chart helps you calculate and visualize your savings goals, particularly for building an emergency fund. Customize it based on your monthly expenses and long-term savings objectives.

Example:

Expense	Monthly Amount	3-Month Goal	6-Month Goal
Rent/Mortgage			
Utilities			
Groceries			
Transportation			
Health Insurance			
Car Insurance			
Misc			
Total			

Acknowledgments

This book wouldn't have been possible without the support, encouragement, and inspiration of so many people along the way.

First and foremost, I want to thank my family and friends for believing in me, even when I doubted myself. Your unwavering love and support gave me the strength to persevere through my own financial challenges and inspired me to share my story with others.

To everyone who shared their own stories of overcoming debt or striving for financial freedom: your courage and resilience remind me that we are never truly alone in our struggles. This book is for you and everyone else fighting to reclaim their financial future.

I also want to express my gratitude to the mentors, authors, and experts whose advice and wisdom helped guide my own journey. Your insights planted the seeds of hope and determination that grew into the strategies and lessons shared in this book.

To my readers, thank you for allowing me to be part of your financial journey. I understand how overwhelming debt can feel, and it is my greatest hope that this book helps you take the first steps toward a brighter future. Your courage to face your financial challenges inspires me every day.

Finally, I want to acknowledge everyone who works tirelessly to create financial literacy resources for people who feel lost, overwhelmed, or ashamed of their financial situations. You are making the world a better place, one empowered person at a time.

This book is a labor of love, born from my own experiences and struggles, and I am so grateful to be able to share it with you. Together, we can rewrite our financial stories and build lives filled with freedom, peace, and hope.

With gratitude,

Razana Gober

Conclusion

Empowering Your Financial Journey

Becoming debt-free is more than just a financial accomplishment—it's a journey of self-discovery, discipline, and empower-ment. It's about reclaiming control of your life and creating a future full of opportunities, peace, and freedom.

I know what it feels like to be buried under the weight of debt. The stress, the sleepless nights, the fear of answering the phone or opening the mail—it can be overwhelming. But I also know how liberating it feels to break free from those burdens.

That's why I wrote this book: to show you that financial freedom isn't just possible—it's within your reach.

What You've Learned

Throughout this book, you've gained the tools and strategies to take control of your finances:

- ◆ You've learned how to create a realistic budget that works for your life.
- ◆ You've explored proven methods, like the Debt Snowball, to pay off debt step by step.
- ◆ You've discovered creative ways to save money, increase your income, and set boundaries.
- ◆ You've prepared yourself to navigate financial challenges and build a secure future for yourself and your family.

Why This Matters

Being debt-free isn't just about the numbers in your bank account. It's about:

- ◆ Emotional Freedom: No more constant stress or anxiety about how to make ends meet.

- Physical and Mental Health: Reduced financial stress means improved overall well-being.
- Stronger Relationships: Money no longer has to be a source of conflict or strain in your relationships.
- Future Opportunities: You can now focus on building wealth, pursuing your passions, and living life on your own terms.

Your Next Steps

1. Take Action Today: Don't wait for the "perfect" moment to start your journey. Begin where you are, with what you have.
2. Stay Consistent: Progress may feel slow at times, but every small step adds up over time.
3. Celebrate Your Wins: Recognize and reward yourself for the milestones you achieve, no matter how small.
4. Share Your Journey: Inspire others by sharing your successes and lessons learned.

You're Not Alone

If you're feeling overwhelmed or unsure where to start, remember that you're not alone. I've been there. I've walked this path, and I know it's not easy—but it's worth it. And you don't have to go it alone. There are communities, resources, and people cheering you on every step of the way.

A Final Word of Encouragement

This journey isn't just about paying off debt. It's about transforming your relationship with money, reclaiming your peace of mind, and unlocking a future full of possibilities.

You have the power to change your financial story, no matter how deep in debt you are or how hopeless it might feel right now. Take a deep breath, believe in yourself, and take that first step. You are capable, you are strong, and you are deserving of the freedom and stability that financial independence brings.

Thank you for letting me be a part of your journey. I'm rooting for you, and I can't wait to see the incredible things you accomplish.

With hope and encouragement,

Razana Gober

About the Author

Razana Gober knows firsthand what it feels like to be overwhelmed by debt. At one point, she was juggling multiple minimum-wage jobs, attending school full-time, and barely making ends meet. She understands the crushing weight of financial stress—the sleepless nights, the endless bills, and the feeling of drowning in a cycle with no way out.

Through relentless determination, hard work, and significant sacrifices, Razana transformed her financial situation. She not only paid off tens of thousands of dollars in debt but also learned the life-changing value of budgeting, perseverance, and making intentional financial choices. Today, she proudly lives debt-free and enjoys the freedom and peace that come with it.

Razana wrote this book because she understands both the struggle of being in over your head and the profound relief of financial freedom. Her mission is to help others find their own path to a debt-free life, offering practical guidance and heartfelt encouragement without judgment or shame.

This book is her way of sharing the lessons she learned, the strategies that worked, and the hope that sustained her along the way. Razana believes everyone deserves to live a life free of financial burdens, and her goal is to empower readers to take control of their finances and reclaim their freedom.

www.ingramcontent.com/pod-product-compliance
Ingram Content Group UK Ltd.
Pitfield, Milton Keynes, MK11 3LW, UK
UKHW021255180426
11947UKWH00011B/795